A
Fres
Aquariums
by Mike Wickham

Fish photos: ©William Zarnick, Animal Graphics
Equipment photos: ©Aquaria, Inc.; Tetra, Inc,; Walmart, Inc.

First Published in the U.S. in 2000 by Dalmatian Press, U.S.A.

Dalmatian Press, 2000
ISBN: 1-57759-369-3

11022A
00 01 02 QWB 10 9 8 7 6 5 4

Introduction

Aquarium fish come from all over the world—primarily from the tropics. Only a few decades ago, almost all were caught in the wild and shipped to importers and dealers throughout the world. These days, though, most species come from commercial fish farms in Florida and Southeast Asia.

Fishkeeping is the second most popular hobby in the world. Only photography has more participants. People keep fish for many reasons. Initially, the brilliant colors and dazzling motions of the fish attract you, but you soon discover that there are other benefits to keeping aquariums:

- Aquariums are relaxing to watch. Studies show that watching fish calms you and lowers your blood pressure.
- Aquariums look great in our homes. A well-decorated aquarium will complement the decor of any room. Aquariums are living furniture.
- Aquariums teach us about nature. They are windows to the natural underwater world.
- Aquariums teach us about science. The deeper you choose to get into the hobby, the more you will come to understand the interactions between animals, plants, and the environment. You will develop a new respect for water, too.

Perhaps the coolest thing about keeping fish as a hobby is that it is easy! It's true. Did you know that if you have to spend more than five or ten minutes per week maintaining your aquarium, you are probably doing something wrong? You can even go on vacation without hiring a fishsitter. It doesn't get quicker or easier than that. Furthermore, if you follow a few simple rules—*all of which are outlined in this book*—you may never lose a fish to anything but old age. (The oldest documented fish lived for 226 years, so you may have your fish for a very long time!) The more you know, the more successful you will be with your hobby. So sit back and do a little reading—preferably before you buy your fish. *A Guide to Freshwater Aquariums* will help you master the basics; a resource list is included at the back of the book for those who want to dig deeper.

Happy fishkeeping!

Mike Wickham

Table of Contents

Basics of Fishkeeping

1. Never buy fish until the aquarium has been set up and running for at least 24 hours.

2. Place your aquarium on a proper aquarium stand—never on a TV or entertainment center.

3. Your filter must provide biological, chemical, and mechanical filtration. A power filter provides all three.

4. Tropical fish require an aquarium heater.

5. Use a water conditioner to remove chlorine from tapwater to make it fish-safe.

6. Learn about *new tank syndrome* before adding fish.

7. Monitor water quality with test kits.

8. Don't overcrowd.

9. Mix compatible species.

10. "Float" new arrivals to prevent temperature shock.

11. Don't overfeed.

12. Offer a variety of foods.

13. Change 20% of the aquarium water every two weeks.

14. Take time to read and learn.

Starter Kits

The easiest way to get started is to buy a kit, but they aren't all equal, and it is important to know what you are getting. Packages may be labeled as "starter kits," "aquarium kits," or even "complete aquarium kits," but no matter how labeled, no kit is complete. There will always be a few other items needed to round out the setup. Minimally, you will need to buy your gravel and decorations separately.

A good starter kit will contain, at least, the following three components:

1. An aquarium

2. A lighting system (preferably a full-hood)

3. A good filtration system (preferably a power filter)

Deluxe kits will add a heater and thermometer, and may offer a fluorescent light (a desirable feature) rather than an incandescent one.

***This Aquaculture brand starter kit contains almost everything you need at a low price.

You must purchase additional supplies and decorations to complete your kit. Use the shopping list on the following page to be sure that you buy all necessary equipment. Check off the items contained in your starter kit, and then find remaining items elsewhere on the store shelves.

Equipment Shopping Lists

Here are the minimum items you need to get started:

[ ] **Aquarium**
[ ] **Aquarium stand**
[ ] **Full-hood with bulb(s)**
[ ] **Power filter**
[ ] **Heater** (may be unnecessary for goldfish)
[ ] **Thermometer**
[ ] **Fish food**
[ ] **Water conditioner**
[ ] **Gravel**
[ ] **Fish net**
[ ] **Background**
[ ] **Plants and decorations**
[ ] **This book!**

> **Warning: NEVER buy fish the same day you buy the equipment!** *Wait at least 24 hours* to be sure that the tank doesn't leak, all equipment is functioning properly, and the water temperature is correct and stable.

You'll need these items to properly maintain your setup:

[ ] **Gravel vacuum**
[ ] **Algae scrubber**
[ ] **Test kits**
[ ] **A "Fish Only" bucket**

The pages that follow will give you full descriptions and buying tips for each item in the list.

Aquariums

Always buy the biggest aquarium you can afford (that will fit in your space). A larger aquarium provides a more stable environment for your fish. A larger aquarium gives schooling species room to swim and territorial species spaces to claim. It takes approximately the same time to maintain a large tank as a small one. Best of all, a large aquarium is more enjoyable because it allows you to keep more beautiful fish!

Most aquariums have a rectangular shape, but you may find hexagonal and other shapes, as well. Rectangular aquariums tend to be the most economical. The main thing to remember about the shape of an aquarium is that wide and low is better than tall and narrow. Tall, narrow aquariums have little surface area to promote the absorption of oxygen. They also have a small footprint that gives fish little room to claim territory. Besides, fish like to swim from side to side, not up and down.

Most aquariums are made of glass or acrylic. (Some mini-tanks are made of cheaper plastics.) Gallon for gallon, glass aquariums tend to be cheaper than acrylic tanks. Acrylic tanks are a bit harder to break than glass ones, but acrylic scratches more easily and requires more caution. Acrylic tanks can also be formed into more unusual shapes.

Don't forget to measure your space at home before you go aquarium shopping!

Mini-Tanks & Fishbowls

Mini-Tanks: Because of their limited space, aquariums of five gallons or less are probably not the best way to begin the hobby of fishkeeping. However, if you allow for their limitations, mini-tanks are great for desktops or other small spaces. The main thing is to be sure to buy a unit that has a light and power filter, and *never* keep more than one inch of fish per gallon, *no matter how many fish are pictured on the box!*

***This Galaxy 5 mini-tank from Regent is well designed, with a built-in filter and light.*

Fishbowls: Many of us became fishkeepers when we won a goldfish at a local carnival and bought a bowl for it. Fishbowls can still be found on store shelves, but they really make a poor choice for keeping most fish. Did you know that goldfish grow over a foot long and can live for 25 years? Well, they can—but not in a fishbowl. There isn't nearly enough room. The fish soon suffocate or die from their own pollution.

One of the few fish that does well in a fishbowl is the male betta. Bettas fight viciously with each other, and their long, flowing fins often make them the target of nips from other species in a mixed aquarium. Many hobbyists keep one of these beautiful fish in a bowl by itself. Bettas have a special chamber in their gills that allows them to gulp a bubble of air from above the water surface and breathe from it. Cramped quarters that would suffocate other fish don't bother bettas at all.

Aquarium Stands

Your aquarium needs proper support. This support must be strong, flat, and level. Wobbly stands or stands that aren't flat can cause your aquarium to twist and break.

The only appropriate place for tanks of ten gallons or more is on a commercial aquarium stand. A full aquarium weighs approximately ten pounds per gallon. You may be able to fit a tiny aquarium or mini-tank on a desktop or countertop, but commercial aquarium stands are better choices for most aquariums. Commercial aquarium stands can safely bear the weight. *Warning: Never place an aquarium of any size on top of a TV or other electrical appliance, or in an entertainment center!*

*** This simple knock-down stand assembles in minutes.

There are many styles of aquarium stands. The simplest are knock-down styles, made of either wrought iron or wood, that can be bolted together using a wrench or socket set. Some styles allow a second aquarium to be placed on a lower shelf.

Pre-assembled cabinet stands are also available. You can store your food, net, and other supplies inside the cabinet and out of view.

Lighting Systems

An aquarium wouldn't be much fun if you couldn't see the fish. A proper lighting system will help you do just that. Many lighting systems completely cover the tank, providing additional benefits: They keep the fish from jumping out. They help keep cats and kids out of the tank. They reduce evaporation.

*** *The easiest way to add light to an aquarium is with a full-hood, such as this one by Perfecto.*

A "full-hood" consists of a plastic cover for your aquarium, with a light unit built in. A hinged door allows access to feed the fish or to perform maintenance on the tank. Full-hoods come with two styles of lighting: incandescent and fluorescent.

Incandescent vs. fluorescent: Incandescent lights use screw-in bulbs, similar to household bulbs. Fluorescent bulbs are long tubes with pins at each end. Incandescent light units cost a bit less, initially, but a fluorescent light is a better buy. Fluorescent bulbs last longer, use less energy, don't produce excessive heat, and provide a brighter, more even distribution of light.

Tip: Incandescent bulbs come in many colors, but you should use only clear, white, or "plant" bulbs. Colored bulbs (red, green, blue, etc.) are unhealthy for fish and plants. Choose fluorescent bulbs designed especially for aquariums to reduce proliferation of ugly algae.

Filtration Basics

Before you choose a filter, you need to understand what filtration is, so that you can choose wisely. Filtration is the process where we pass aquarium water through filter media. The filter media traps waste, but allows the water to pass. Later, when the media reaches capacity, you discard the dirty media and replace it with new.

There are three types of filtration—mechanical, biological, and chemical. For best results, your filter system must provide all three.

1. Mechanical filtration: When most of us think of filtration, mechanical filtration is what we picture. It is the physical straining of *solid* wastes from the water. Fish feces, uneaten food, and other debris, are trapped by the filter media.

2. Biological filtration: Solid wastes aren't the only problem, though. There are also *dissolved* wastes. Biological filtration takes advantage of natural, helpful bacteria to break down some of these wastes—particularly the ammonia that is excreted by fish. Of the three types of filtration, biological is probably the most important, because ammonia poisons fish quickly.

3. Chemical filtration: We place activated carbon into our filters to provide chemical filtration. Activated carbon removes *dissolved* wastes by bonding with them chemically. Once the chemical bonds are saturated with waste, the media must be replaced. There is no way to tell when this occurs, so replace it monthly.

The solution to pollution is dilution. Filtration helps us maintain clear, clean water, *but it's not enough!* Filters can only do so much. Regular, partial water changes complete the job. Water changes remove dissolved wastes and replace depleted trace elements. Change 20% of your water every other week to keep a healthy tank.

Filtration Systems

Your filter system is vital to the health of your aquarium. It removes waste and it oxygenates the water. Without a filter, you would be unable to keep many fish in your aquarium, because they would soon die from their own pollution or lack of oxygen. There are many styles of filters on the market. Remember that your choice needs to provide mechanical, biological, and chemical filtration. It may take more than one filter to do the job.

Power filters: *The best choice for most hobbyists is a power filter.* It hangs on the back of your aquarium, and a built-in motor draws water from the tank and pumps it through the filter media. The water then flows through a chute that returns it, waterfall style, to the tank. Power filters are simple to maintain. When filter cartridges are dirty, you toss them and replace with a new, clean cartridge.

***Power filters, such as those by Aqua-Tech *and* Whisper, *are the best choice for most hobbyists. Choose the right size for your tank. Example: A filter that says "5-15" is for tanks from 5 to 15 gallons.*

Power filters provide all three types of filtration—mechanical, biological, and chemical. However, since the helpful bacteria that provide biological filtration grow on the filter media, when you discard the dirty media, you also throw away much of your biological filtration. Some models contain permanent filter media (such as sponges or *Bio-Wheels®*). These models retain more helpful bacteria between filter cleanings.

Undergravel filters: This style of filter works, but is losing popularity. It consists of a perforated plate that goes beneath the gravel. A riser tube in each rear corner contains an air stone, powered by an air pump that sits outside the aquarium.

Undergravel filters draw water down through the gravel bed, where fish droppings and other detritus are trapped. Helpful bacteria colonize the gravel and break down ammonia and nitrite. *Since undergravel filters use gravel as the filter media, the regular use of a gravel vacuum is essential!* Undergravel filters are poor choices for heavily decorated aquariums, since the decorations obstruct the gravel bed and prevent easy vacuuming.

Undergravel filters provide good mechanical and biological filtration, but no chemical filtration—unless you buy optional carbon cartridges that fit on top the riser tubes to provide minimal chemical filtration. You can add a small power filter for more chemical filtration.

***This Aqua-Tech undergravel filter fits beneath the gravel. Cover the filter plate 1.5-2" (4-5cm) deep with 3/16" (5mm) diameter gravel.

Canister filters: Most canister filters sit beneath the aquarium and connect with hoses, but one model hangs on the back, much like a power filter. Canisters provide mechanical, chemical, and limited biological filtration.

Air pumps: Air bubbles add beauty to a tank. Bubbles disturb the surface to increase oxygen exchange. Air pumps can power filters, operate ornaments, or provide supplemental circulation and oxygenation.

Heating Systems

Aquarium heaters

Maintaining a stable temperature is important because it reduces stress and helps prevent disease. Clamp-on heaters attach to the back of the aquarium and are the cheapest. Submersible models, which attach to the inside aquarium glass with suction cups, are more childproof because they are completely submersible, including part of the electrical cord.

***These Aquaculture *and* Whisper *aquarium heaters have automatic thermostats. Once set, they will prevent temperatures from dropping below the desired level.*

Thermometers

A thermometer is necessary to calibrate your heater and to know the temperature of your aquarium. Liquid crystal thermometers stick on the outside glass and are most accurate. Floating thermometers have the advantage of being easily moved to test the temperature of a bucket of water.

Fish Foods

Types of Food

Dry foods offer long shelf life and easy storage. (It's best to replace dry foods after a few months or a year, though, as they do go stale eventually.) Dry foods are convenient and less messy to feed.

Flakes: Dry flake fish foods are easily the most popular style of food. Most starter kits include a small supply of "staple" flakes as the first food for your fish. Staple flakes provide good basic nutrition for a broad range of tropical fish species. Look for color enhancing flakes to bring out the brightest colors in your fish. Special flakes are also available for goldfish and cichlids.

***TetraMin *and* TetraFin *are basic flakes for tropical fish and goldfish, respectively.*

Pellets and tablets: Pelleted foods come in floating and sinking forms. Floating pellets help surface-feeding species get their fair share of food. Sinking pellets and tablet foods target bottom feeders. "Food sticks" are elongated pellets. Some pellets may cloud your water, so don't overdo them. Look for special algae tablets to supplement the diet of plecostomus and other algae-eating fish.

Freeze-dried foods: Flakes and pellets are made from an amalgamation of cooked ingredients. Freeze-dried foods consist of whole aquatic insect larvae and crustaceans in dried form, resembling more closely the diet of wild fish. Freeze-dried bloodworms, tubifex worms, and shrimp are most popular.

***Watch your fish go crazy for freeze-dried bloodworms and tubifex worms!

Specialty foods: You'll also find dry foods created for specific varieties of fish, including cichlids and bettas. There is even a floating food stick for turtles and aquatic African frogs. (Turtles eat fish and frogs, though, so don't keep them together!)

Frozen foods: Bloodworms, brine shrimp, tubifex worms, and other tiny aquatic animals can be purchased in frozen form. Frozen foods are sold in "flat-packs" or trays of mini-cubes. Mini-cubes are most convenient—simply pop them out of the tray and into your tank.

Live foods: Create a feeding frenzy by offering live foods. All fish love them. Some species *require* them! Be sure you know the dietary requirements of your fish before purchase.

Choosing the Right Diet

While it's true that many species of fish may live a long time on a diet of staple flakes alone, that diet would not be ideal for most fish. Match your choices of foods to the feeding habits of the fish you keep.

Carnivores and herbivores: Fish don't all eat the same thing. Carnivores want meat. Herbivores want algae and vegetation. Omnivores want a little of each.

Most of the carnivorous fish that we keep will readily take commercial dry foods, and can be offered freeze-dried foods, pellets, and flakes that meet their dietary requirements. Some carnivores, however, require food that is either live, or close to it. Peacock spiny eels, for example, won't touch flake foods, but may take frozen or freeze-dried.

Herbivores can have their diet supplemented with algae tablets. Consider offering algae tablets to plecostomus and other algae-eating fish, after they clear away the initial bit of algae. These fish can die without ample vegetation in the diet.

Surface-dwellers and bottom-feeders: Food is of little use when it's out of reach. Hatchetfish will never feed from the bottom and require food that floats at least long enough for them to get their fair share. Floating pellets are useless to some bottom dwellers, too.

Day or night: Feedings should match the activity cycle of your fish. If your daily feedings are light (as they should be), the food will be long gone when night-dwellers come out to eat. Consider offering a small feeding to such fish, when you turn out the lights. The plecostomus is a good example of a fish that often starves this way.

Chemicals

Water Conditioner: Municipalities add chlorine to the water supply to kill germs, but chlorine also destroys the gill membranes of fish. Unless you draw water from your own private well, you need to neutralize the chlorine to make the water safe for aquatic life. Buy a dechlorinating water conditioner to do the job.

Chloramine is sometimes added to the water instead of chlorine. It is more dangerous because it breaks down into chlorine and ammonia. All dechlorinating water conditioners handle the chlorine, but not the ammonia. Special water conditioners are necessary to handle both. You will also require a compatible ammonia test kit.

***Water conditioners and test kits

Water test kits: Just because water is clear doesn't mean it is safe for fish. Smart hobbyists keep test kits on hand to monitor water quality. Most important are pH and ammonia kits. A *pH* kit tells you if your water is acidic or alkaline. *Ammonia* and *nitrite* kits measure fish waste.

Test kits don't just help you understand your tapwater. They also come in handy if disease appears. Poor water quality is the number one stressor of fish. Stress makes fish more susceptible to disease. When fish are sick, you should always test the water before medicating, to rule out water quality problems!

Note: Tapwater varies by geographical location. Other treatments and tests may be necessary in some areas.

Cleaning Supplies

Gravel vacuum: This device makes fishkeeping easy! You should change 20% of your water every other week. The gravel vacuum removes the crud from your gravel, while it siphons out water for your regular partial water changes. You kill two birds with one stone. It is the quickest and easiest way to maintain your tank!

***The indispensable gravel vacuum comes in many sizes and styles.

Algae scrubber pad: Over time, algae will tend to grow on the glass. A scrubber pad clears it away, so you can see your fish. Hand-held pads are the best, fitting easily into corners. Handle-mounted models reach deeper, but are less maneuverable. *Warning: Never substitute household sponges or scrubbers. They are treated with toxic chemicals! Use only aquarium algae scrubber pads. Warning: Some algae pads scratch acrylic tanks. If your tank is acrylic, buy a pad that is acrylic safe!*

"Fish Only" bucket: A good five-gallon bucket comes in quite handy during water changes. You probably have buckets at home, but *buy a new one and label it "Fish Only! No Soap!"* Then, be sure everyone in the household knows not to use it for anything else. Traces of soap will kill your fish!

Decorations

Gravel: It comes in many colors, but it is not merely a decoration! Gravel provides a substrate to anchor plants, and harbors helpful bacteria that break down waste.

Small stones are better than large. Choose gravel with a particle size of 1/8 to 1/4 inch diameter. If the stones are larger, so are the spaces between them. Large spaces allow food to fall between the gravel—out of reach of the fish—where it will decay and pollute.

Choose dark colors to bring out the color of your fish. Buy enough gravel to make a layer 1.5-2" deep. Use the table below as a guideline:

Tank size (gals):	5	10	20H	29	55
lbs. Gravel:	10	15	20	30	60

Plants: Besides the decorative appearance, plants provide cover for your fish. Adult fish can hide from bullies and fry (baby fish) can hide from hungry adults! Buy a mix of sizes for a natural look. Plant taller specimens in the back for optimal view.

Plastic plants don't die, don't get eaten, and don't need pruning. Many people find them easier to maintain. Still, I prefer live plants. They are more natural and move more with the water flow. Since they grow, the scenery in the aquarium changes over time for a more dynamic display. Live plants provide a source of food for some fish, and they remove some waste nutrients from the water. They may even provide a bit of oxygen. Of course, they may require pruning and fertilization.

Background: An aquarium background enhances the beauty of your aquarium, while hiding electrical cords and airlines. Scenes come printed on rolled plastic sheets. Merely tape them to the back of your aquarium.

Rocks: A few strategically positioned rocks can liven up your aquarium. Be sure to buy rocks that are aquarium safe. You may even find artificial rocks on the store shelf.

Driftwood: Natural driftwood may leach tannins that discolor the water. Look for artificial driftwood. You can't tell it from the real thing.

Ceramics: Castles, treasure chests, "no fishing" signs, bubbling divers, and other ornaments are readily available for those who like them.

Air curtain: You can use an air pump to power airstones and bubble-wands for decorative curtains of bubbles.

Miscellaneous

Fish net: Use a 3" net for bowls and a 5" net for the typical fish in a community aquarium.

Beginner's book: Fish plus water does not necessarily equal success. Fish are living things. If you want to be successful at keeping them alive, you need to arm yourself with knowledge. This book provides the basics for you. If you want a deeper understanding, and the ability to keep more difficult species, you need to do further research. Read as many books as you can. I suggest starting with the *KISS (Keep It Simple Series) Guide to Freshwater Aquariums*. I know the author personally, and he's a very cool guy!

Putting It All Together

Yes, some assembly is required! You will have many brands of products when you arrive home. *Always read all manufacturer's instructions before assembly.* Even after you do so, assembly may appear to be a daunting task. Here are some unified instructions to help you along.

1. Test the tank for leaks. Glass aquariums are inspected before shipment, and leaks are rare, but damage can result in transit. To test for leaks, move the aquarium to a flat, level surface (preferably with easy drainage), and fill the tank with water. Be very careful not to splash a single drop outside the tank! Let it stand at least thirty minutes and inspect for leaks. If satisfied, use your gravel vac or a plastic dipper to remove the water. *Warning: Never move an aquarium that contains water! Damage may result!*

2. Position the aquarium stand. Pick a location that is flat and level. Leave enough room behind to hang filters and for electrical cords. Use shims to make the stand level or to prevent wobbles on a floor that isn't quite flat.

3. Clean the aquarium glass with plain water and a paper towel. Never use soap! Soap kills fish!

4. Attach your aquarium background to the outside back of your tank with cellophane tape.

5. Center the aquarium on the stand. Check again to be sure there is enough space behind for hanging filters.

6. Rinse your aquarium gravel and pour it into the tank. Place the gravel into a bucket and use a garden hose to run water through it until it rinses clean. Natural gravels require more rinsing than colored gravels. Slope the gravel so that it is slightly higher in back. This gives more depth for planting, and helps bits of debris drift toward the front for easy removal. *Note: If you bought an undergravel filter, install the filter plate and riser-tubes before putting gravel in the tank!*

7. Install heavy decorations. Large rocks, driftwood, and ceramic ornaments are more easily installed now. Installing later may overflow the aquarium as the ornament displaces water.

8. Fill the aquarium. Place a coffee saucer on the bottom of the tank. Then, pour the water onto it to avoid disturbing the gravel. Use your "fish only" bucket or a garden hose to fill. If you use the latter, rinse it out first. Try to mix hot and cold water to achieve the ideal temperature of 75-78°F (24-26°C) for tropical fish, or 70-75°F (21-24°C) for goldfish. Fill until the water reaches the bottom of the top aquarium frame.

9. Dechlorinate. Use your water conditioner to remove chlorine from the tapwater, making it safe for fish.

10. Install plants and remaining decorations. Decorating is an art. Position items to suit your taste. Try to avoid unnatural symmetry. Keeping taller objects to the rear allows for a clear view.

11. Install your filter. Power filters hang on the back of the tank, with an intake tube protruding into the water. Follow the manufacturer's instructions for the model you chose. Generally, you must fill the filter box with water before plugging in the filter. Plug in the filter and allow it to begin its work.

12. Install the heater. Some models clamp on the back of the tank; others are completely submersible. Follow the manufacturer's instructions! *Warning: Do **not** plug in the heater at this time!*

> *Warning: A hot heater will burn you and can shatter when it hits cold water. A hot heater can cause a fire. Never plug in a heater that is not already installed in water. Always unplug and allow your heater to cool before removing it from the aquarium.*

13. Install your thermometer. Attach liquid crystal thermometers to the outside glass, using the adhesive strip. You can position the thermometer anywhere that it doesn't obstruct your view. Floating thermometers go inside the tank. Gently bump the thermometer into a front corner to keep it from drifting.

14. Install the full-hood. Before installing your lighting system, you will need to punch out, or cut out, spaces in the rear plastic strip to allow room for any filters or heaters hanging on the back of the tank. You also may need to snap pegs off the bottom of the hood to get the right fit for your brand of aquarium. Follow the manufacturer's instructions.

15. Calibrating your heater: If 15 minutes has passed since you installed your heater, go ahead and plug it in. (This allowed the heater parts to become the same temperature as the aquarium water.) Look at the pilot light. Is it on? If so, turn the heater down, until the pilot light just kicks off. If, instead, the pilot light was off when you plugged in, turn the heater up, until the pilot light just kicks on. At this point your heater is calibrated for the *current* water temperature. If your *desired* temperature is different, turn the heater up or down a bit, and then check back in an hour to fine tune it. Fine tune until you achieve the correct stable temperature. For most heaters, a 1/8 turn of the control knob will make a 2°F (1°C) change. Heaters are fully automatic. Once set, they won't allow the temperature to fall below the desired temperature. Of course, they can't prevent the tank from getting warmer on a hot day.

16. Wait 24 hours before buying fish! Never buy your fish the same day you buy the tank! You need to be sure that the equipment is functioning properly, that the tank doesn't leak, and that the temperature is stable before you buy fish.

17. Run a pH test. Let the filter run a few hours to oxygenate the water. Then, run a pH test to establish a baseline. Most fish prefer a pH around 7.0 (neutral), but 6.8-7.4 is okay for a new tank. If necessary, use chemicals to adjust the pH. See the section on water chemistry for more details.

You are ready for your first batch of fish! Nothing is more fun than fish shopping, but it's not easy work. There are too many great fish and there is not enough room in your tank for all of them! *Read the section on cycling your tank* **before** *you buy fish!*

Making Tapwater Safe

Chlorine and chloramines: Though tapwater is safe for drinking, most is unsafe for fish without first being treated. City water treatment plants add chlorine to kill germs to make water safe for drinking. However, chlorine will destroy the gill membranes of your fish and must be neutralized.

The easiest way to remove chlorine is with a simple dechlorinating water conditioner. Follow the directions on the bottle (usually in drops per gallon or teaspoons per ten gallons) to neutralize chlorine instantly.

Some water treatment plants add another chemical that combines with chlorine to form chloramines. Chloramines are a little trickier to deal with. Normal dechlorinators will remove the chlorine component of chloramine, but leave behind toxic ammonia in the process. Check with your local salesperson to see if you need to neutralize chlorine or chloramines.

If your local water supply contains chloramines, you need to buy a special water conditioner that neutralizes both chlorine and ammonia. (Make sure your ammonia test kit is compatible with the product.) Alternately, you can use a regular dechlorinator and add some ammonia-removing chips to your filter.

Adjusting your pH: The ideal pH for most fish is 7.0 (between 6.8-7.4 is fine), but water may not come out of the tap in that range. When you first fill your aquarium, give an hour to aerate, then test the pH. You can use commercial chemicals to adjust the pH, if necessary. Most brands contain sodium bicarbonate (baking soda) to raise pH, and sodium biphosphate to lower pH.

Note: Adjustment of pH is usually not necessary when making partial water changes.

New Tank Syndrome

Fishkeeping is an art and a science. This section explains the part of the science that is most important. *If you don't understand how to "cycle" your aquarium, you will almost certainly lose fish to "new tank syndrome."*

It may seem to defy logic, but your fish are more at risk in a sparkling new, clean tank, than in an old dirty one. You see, your fish excrete ammonia as waste. This ammonia would quickly build up and poison your fish, if it were not for helpful bacteria that neutralize it. Unfortunately, a brand new aquarium does not yet have these "good guy" bacteria. So, you must take precautions.

The Nitrogen Cycle

Here's how it works: The fish begin excreting *ammonia* as soon as you put them in the tank. The ammonia level begins to climb in the absence of helpful bacteria. Simultaneously, helpful *Nitrosomonas* bacteria will begin to colonize the aquarium. After a week or so, the bacteria should develop a population large enough to break down all the toxic ammonia.

The process doesn't stop there, though. The ammonia is broken down into *nitrite,* which is still toxic to your fish! Another group of helpful bacteria—the *Nitrobacter*—will develop to work on the nitrite. It will take another week or more for them to break down the nitrite into *nitrate*.

Nitrate is relatively harmless. It must accumulate in very high levels to become a problem. Your regular partial water changes prevent this from happening.

The process of converting ammonia to nitrite to nitrate is known as the *nitrogen cycle*. We refer to the process as *cycling the aquarium*.

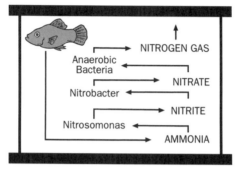

***The Nitrogen Cycle*

Safely Cycling Your Aquarium

If you start with too many fish, they will poison themselves with their own ammonia! The solution is simple. *Start with fewer fish—no more than 1/2" of fish per gallon of water.* The rest can be added later.

Starting with fewer fish means less ammonia will be produced. The idea is to keep ammonia levels low enough to prevent them from killing the fish. Yet, there will be enough ammonia to fuel the growth of those necessary helpful bacteria. (The fish will always produce ammonia, but, after the tank has cycled, you won't know it because the bacteria will break it down as quickly as the fish produce it.)

It is normal for your aquarium to become cloudy during the cycling stage. This cloudiness will dissipate as the cycling is complete. It is not necessary to change or treat water during this stage.

After the tank has cycled (both ammonia and nitrite have risen and fallen back to zero), you will be able to add the rest of your fish to bring the maximum load to 1" of fish per gallon. How will you know when the tank has cycled? This is where your ammonia and nitrite test kits come in. There is no way to tell if your tank has cycled by looking at it, and the timeline is different for every aquarium. You must run tests to monitor the cycling of your aquarium.

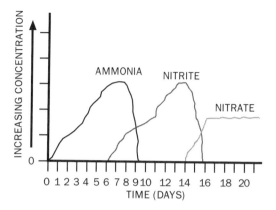

*** *This graph shows the cycling time of a typical aquarium, but each tank is different. Use ammonia and nitrite test kits to confirm the status of your aquarium.*

Patience is the key! If you try to rush the cycling process, if you try to put too many fish in at once, or add too many fish too soon, ammonia and nitrite levels will skyrocket and may kill all of your fish!

Most tanks will see ammonia climb for one week after adding the first batch of fish. Then, detectable ammonia levels will drop back to zero, but nitrite levels will climb for another week or so, before they, too, drop back to zero. The process may take longer than two weeks, though. Each aquarium is different. Only your test kits can confirm the status of the cycle in your aquarium.

What should you do, if your test kit shows high ammonia or nitrite levels? It depends. If the fish look fine, do nothing. Mother Nature will soon correct the problem with helpful bacteria. However, if the fish are stressed or dying, consider 1) changing some water to dilute the ammonia or nitrite, 2) adding ammonia-adsorbing chips to the filter box, 3) buying a bacterial enzyme product to quickly remove ammonia, or 4) adding 1 tsp. of aquarium salt per gallon of water to neutralize the toxicity of the nitrite. (Salt doesn't remove nitrite, it only makes it less toxic.)

Water Chemistry

Water is the prime ingredient in the aquatic environment. We don't think much about water—it has no color, no taste, no odor—but there's more to it than meets the eye, tongue, and nose. Water is the basic building block of life. Understanding water helps us understand our aquarium.

pH: We measure pH on a scale of 0 to 14. A pH of 7.0 is neutral. Higher readings are alkaline; lower readings are acidic. Each 1-point change in pH represents a tenfold change. So, a pH of 6.0 is ten times more acidic than a pH of 7.0, and a pH of 8.0 is 100 times more alkaline than a pH of 6.0.

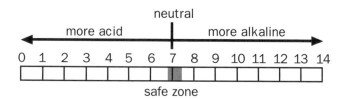

***You can keep most species of fish happy by keeping your pH around 7.0 (neutral). Anywhere from 6.8-7.4 is acceptable, however.

pH affects most chemical and biological processes. Why is it important? For starters, if the pH is too high or low, it can burn your fish. But mainly pH is important for the following reasons:

- Ammonia is more toxic in alkaline water. As the pH drops below 7.0, toxic ammonia (NH_3) begins to convert to less toxic ammonium (NH_4^{++}). So, a higher pH can be more dangerous. However...
- Biological filtration fails when the pH drops below 6.4. When this happens, ammonium builds up. Fortunately, since the pH is low it is the less toxic form. This is dangerous because a sudden upward shift in pH (such as from a long overdue water change) will convert the ammonium into highly toxic ammonia! Use regular water changes to prevent this.

Ammonia and nitrite: See the section on *new tank syndrome* for a fully detailed discussion of these two water quality parameters. Ammonia and nitrite tests are especially helpful to the aquarist cycling a brand new tank. Ammonia and nitrite should not be detectable in well-established aquariums, but I highly recommend that you run both tests any time disease or stress is apparent.

Nitrate: Since nitrate is only toxic in very high quantities, there is generally no need to test for it. Use regular partial water changes to prevent it from building up.

Water hardness: This measurement relates to the amount of calcium and magnesium dissolved in your water. In some geographical areas, where limestone bedrock is prevalent, the water hardness may be quite high. Most hobbyists needn't worry about this parameter, however. If you want to test, look for *general hardness (GH)* test kits.

Carbonate hardness: Buffers are dissolved chemicals that help maintain a stable pH. In water, carbonates and bicarbonates are of chief concern. In some geographical areas, particularly those with soft or acidic water, it may be necessary to add sodium bicarbonate to buffer the water. Look for *carbonate hardness (KH)* or *alkalinity* test kits. Again, most hobbyists needn't worry about this parameter.

Test kits: Testing your water is easy and test kits are readily available. Most kits work the same way. You start by adding aquarium water to a vial. Then, you add a certain number of drops of reagent to the water, and compare the color change to a chart. Some kits require you to wait a specified number of seconds or minutes before comparing the color reading. Follow the manufacturer's instructions. There is really no excuse for not testing your water, when the procedure is so fast and easy.

Adjusting pH: The ideal pH for most fish is around 7.0 (neutral). If your pH is below 6.8, or above 7.4, you may want to adjust it. Your dealer sells chemicals to do so.

If you read in a book that a fish's native waters have a pH of 6.8 and yours is 7.0, don't waste your time adjusting the pH. Your water is already in the safe range. Perfection is not necessary. Fish can tolerate a fairly broad range of pH. What they don't tolerate are sudden changes.

If your local tapwater contains natural buffers (substances that stabilize pH), you may find that any changes you make to the pH will undo themselves within a day. Bouncing the pH up and down is more dangerous than leaving it stable at a less than perfect reading.

Any adjustments should be done slowly. Never adjust the pH more than one full point in a day. Always start by adding less chemical than you think you need. Then, test to see how much change it made, and adjust the dosage accordingly. Each tank is different, so even manufacturer's recommendations may not apply to your tank!

Removing ammonia: If ammonia tests high, but the fish look fine, do nothing. Helpful bacteria will develop to solve the problem. However, if the ammonia is high and the fish are stressed or dying, consider changing some water to dilute the ammonia, adding ammonia-removing chips to your filter, or dosing with a bacterial enzyme product available from your dealer.

Removing nitrite: If nitrite is high, but the fish look fine, do nothing. Helpful bacteria will develop to control the nitrite. If the fish are stressed or dying, you can change some water to dilute the nitrite, but an easier solution is to add 1 tsp. of aquarium salt per gallon. The salt won't remove the nitrite, but it will neutralize the toxicity of it. (This level of salt will not hurt any fish.)

How Many Fish Will Fit?

There are so many dazzling fish species that you will be tempted to buy too many, but overcrowding kills fish! Don't overcrowd! Overcrowding results in poisonous pollution, stunted growth, poor coloration, wounds from territorial disputes, and it facilitates the spread of disease.

> **Limit yourself to no more than one inch (2.5 cm) of fish per gallon of water.** (Do not count the tail when you measure.) If you have a ten gallon tank, that means you can keep ten 1-inch fish, or five 2-inch fish in it.
> *Note: Remember to cycle your new tank with only 1/2" of fish per gallon, and add the rest after the tank cycles.*

Warning: The above 1-inch-per-gallon rule applies *only* to typical "community-sized" fish. That is, it applies to fish up to three inches in length. The rules are quite different for larger fish! When a fish grows, it's not only the length that changes—it's also the width and height. So, a five-inch fish is actually 5 times as long, 5 times as wide, and 5 times as high as a one-inch fish. In other words, it is *125 times* as large as the one-inch fish (5x5x5)! Use the table below for larger fish.

A fish this size:	1"	2"	4"	6"	12"
Equals this many 1" fish:	1	8	64	216	1728
Needs this many gallons of water:	1	2	5	10+	50+

***Five one-inch fish do not equal one five-inch fish!

Compatibility Guide

Kissing gouramies really do kiss, but not all fish get along so swimmingly. Be sure to pick species that will mix well in your aquatic community.

There are many reasons why fish may fight, including bickering over territory, potential mates, and food supplies. Fortunately, most species sold in the aquarium trade are for "community tanks" and get along quite well. *Research each species before you buy it. Big fish eat little fish. Even big* peaceful *fish eat little fish!*

Schooling behavior: Some species live solitary lives, while others prefer to be part of the crowd. Species that like to school should always be kept as a group. Otherwise, their behavior may change. Tiger barbs are a good example. They mix well with most other fish, but they like to chase each other around. If you have too few tiger barbs, they will chase and nip the other fish instead. *Buy at least three of any schooling species. Six is even better.*

Territorial behavior: While schooling species will roam the entire aquarium, other fish like to stake out a territory to call home. They may claim a rock, the underside of a piece of driftwood, or a corner of the aquarium. If you place too many territorial fish in your aquarium, serious fights may ensue over the limited space.

Surface-dwellers and bottom-dwellers: Picking a good mix of top, midwater, and bottom dwellers will give your aquarium a more interesting appearance. It will also spread territory more evenly between all inhabitants to avoid disputes.

Time of activity: Before you buy a fish, find out when it likes to sleep. If you buy all nocturnal (night dwelling) species, there won't be much to watch during the daytime!

Choosing Healthy Fish

Before you buy your first fish, learn the visual cues that show a fish to be healthy. Avoid buying a fish—even a healthy looking one—from aquariums that have other sick or dying fish in them. (The section on *stress and disease* will tell you how to spot a sick fish.)

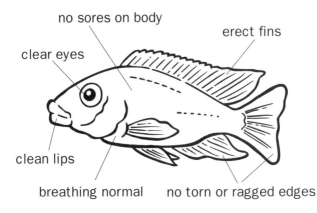

***The signs of a healthy fish.

Look for erect fins with no splits, tears, or rotted edges. However, note that some fish, such as the popular algae-eating plecostomus, normally keep their fins folded against the body. Also look for clear eyes, full (but not bloated) stomachs, and skin that is colorful and lacking in dull patches.

Fish with bloody or slimy patches on the skin or fins should be avoided. Do not buy fish that have *ich* infections. When your fish has ich, it has tiny white dots on the skin and fins that appear as though someone took a salt shaker and sprinkled the fish.

Watch for a fish that displays a good level of activity and interest in life. Again, there are some species, such as the plecostomus, that normally spend the day hiding.

Popular Varieties

The "community tank,"—a tank consisting of a mixture of small, peaceful fish—is what most people keep. Here are some popular species that generally mix well together, along with some helpful hints.

Algae-eaters: (pronounced AL-jee, by the way) Save yourself some work by adding fish that help keep the glass clean. Otocinclus are the best choice for the community tank. They stay small and are active during the day. Use one for each five to ten gallons. Plecostomus are also excellent algae-eaters, but may grow to well over a foot in length. Only one plecostomus per tank is necessary. Avoid the Chinese algae-eater. It eats little algae and may attack the other fish when it grows, feeding off their body slime.

***Tiger barb

Barbs: This highly active group of fishes fare best when kept in schools. Cherry barbs and rosy barbs are quite peaceful. Tiger barbs may get nippy, unless you keep at least six. (They like to chase each other, but lacking that, will chase the other fish, instead.) Tiger barbs will nip long-finned fish.

Botias & loaches: (bo-TEE-uz) The yo-yo loach is a handsome scavenger, mostly seen at night. It can help rid a tank of snails. Kuhlii loaches (A.K.A. "coolie") are peaceful, reclusive, and eel-shaped.

Catfish: The various corydoras catfish are excellent scavengers and are active during the day—a rarity amongst catfishes. They prefer to school, so keep at least one per five gallons. The pictus catfish is a beautiful, spotted predator. Mix it only with fish of similar size.

***A corydoras catfish

Cichlids: (SICK-lids) Most cichlids are too aggressive for the community tank. (One type, the Jack Dempsey, was named after a famous fighter for a reason!) Angelfish and kribensis are exceptions that mix with most fish. Oscars are relatively peaceful, too, but quickly grow to over a foot.

***Long-fin zebra danio

Danios: (DAN-ee-ohs) Zebra danios and pearl danios are wonderful fish for the community tank. They never stop moving! Keep them in a small school.

Spiny Eels: These interesting fish are a poor choice for the community tank because they require live, or at least frozen, foods. Flake foods will go untouched.

***Dwarf African frog

Frogs: The dwarf African frog is an amusing addition to your tank. They even eat flake food!

Glassfish: Glassfish are brackish water fish. They fare poorly without the addition of salt to the water. Avoid painted glass fish—their fluorescent colors are artificial and will eventually wear off.

Goldfish: The Chinese domesticated the goldfish centuries ago. Selective breeding has given us many forms and colors. Did you know that all goldfish start out brown, and then change? Color changes may even occur in adult goldfish. Goldfish can grow to over a foot in length, so allow them plenty of room. Goldfish are great for ornamental garden ponds. They will winter over if the pond is deep enough to prevent complete freezing.

***Red cap oranda

Goldfish varieties:
- The single-tailed *comet* goldfish is most well known, and is seen in orange, white, brown, or in combinations of those colors.
- The *shubunkin* is a calico (orange, white, blue, and black) comet.
- The *fantail* sports a fat body and double tail.
- The *black moor* is all black with bulgy eyes.
- The *oranda* is a fantail with a raspberry growth on the head. The red cap oranda, with a white body and red hat, is most well known.
- The *lionhead* is an oranda without a dorsal fin.

Gouramies: (go-RAH-meez) Kissing gouramies are the most well-known fish in this group, and they really do kiss! Buy two to see the kissing behavior, which they use to mark territorial boundaries. Dwarf gouramies are a good choice for the community tank. They come in several strains of red and blue and grow to around 2". Gold gouramies and blue gouramies are different strains of another species. They are a bit more aggressive and grow larger—up to 6". Keep only one or two gouramies of any species in your tank to reduce territorial fighting. The male betta (Siamese fighting fish) is related to the gouramies. Bettas fight with each other. Keep only one per tank.

***Male fancy guppy

Guppies: Guppies are one of the earliest tropical aquarium fish, though the fancy guppies of today look nothing like the original fish. (These days, the original fish sells as "feeder guppies" to feed other fish!) Large fins and bright colors are the result of selective breeding. Males have larger fins and more color than females. Guppies are livebearers, so keep at least two females for each male. (Too many males and the females never get a chance to rest!) Don't mix guppies with fin nippers!

Knifefish: The black ghost knife fish is popular but grows to over a foot long and is too large for the typical community. They also fare poorly on a diet of flakes. Live and frozen foods should be considered necessary.

Koi: The Chinese first domesticated this carp, but the Japanese deserve credit for the fantastic colors seen in them today. Small koi are sometimes kept in aquariums, but this fish, which reaches a length of two to three feet, is best reserved for the garden pond.

Minnows: The white cloud mountain minnow is a small, danio-like fish. Juveniles have an iridescent stripe which has earned them the name of "poor man's neon." This fish prefers cooler water, under 75°F. Adult size is under 2".

Mollies: These livebearing fishes do best when you add one or two teaspoons of aquarium salt per gallon, and keep the temperature between 78°-82°F. (Don't worry. The salt won't hurt your other fish.) They also lean toward an herbivorous diet. The pure black mollies are a spectacular strain developed from, believe it or not, a wild gray fish. Large sailfin varieties are also popular, especially the gold sailfin, which is a gaudy yellow-orange. Keep at least two females for each male.

***Black lyretail molly

Platies: (plat-eez) Peaceful, hardy, and loaded with color... What more could you ask of a fish? Platies are livebearers, so keep two females for each male. "Wag" platies have black fins, "tuxedo" platies have black sides, and "crescent" platies have black at the base of the tail.

***Red wag platy

Rainbowfish: These fish prefer a bit of salt in the water. A teaspoon of aquarium salt per gallon will do, and will even help prevent disease in your other fish. Rainbows are active and like to school. Males tend to be more colorful.

Sharks: Not true sharks, these fish get their name from the shape of the dorsal fin. Bala and iridescent sharks are midwater schoolers and are active during the day. Keep them in groups. They are peaceful, but grow to over a foot and may not be the best choice for your community! Red-tail and rainbow sharks are popular scavengers, active mostly at night. Red-tail and rainbow sharks fight amongst themselves, though, so keep only one per tank.

***Rainbow shark

Swordtails: The males of this livebearing fish, sprout a sword-shaped extension on the tail. Males joust with each other. It is usually best not to keep more than one or two males per tank, and always with at least two females per male. Like platies, swordtails have been selectively bred into many bright color strains.

***Serpae tetra

Tetras: Many species are included in this large group of fishes. The most popular is surely the neon tetra, with its amazing fluorescent colors. Glow-light tetras also display iridescent colors. Black tetras sport an unusual body shape and serpae (SER-pee) tetras are cherry red. Beware "blueberry" and "raspberry" tetras. They have been dyed and the colors will eventually fade.

Sample Communities

If you would like a helping hand, here are some tried-and-true communities that you can mix in a standard *ten gallon aquarium*. Use the fish from the batch in the first column to cycle the aquarium. After the tank has cycled, add the fish in the second column to fill out the tank. Don't rush the process, or you may lose fish from high ammonia levels. See the section on *new tank syndrome* for a full explanation.

TROPICAL FISH

1st Batch	2nd Batch
3 red wag platies	3 neon tetras
3 tiger barbs	1 rainbow shark

1st Batch	2nd Batch
3 zebra danios	3 cherry barbs
2 corydoras catfish	1 male dwarf gourami

1st Batch	2nd Batch
3 pearl danios	2 otocinclus
2 pair fancy guppies	2 dwarf African frogs

1st Batch	2nd Batch
3 assorted platies	2 corydoras catfish
3 white cloud minnows	2 neon rainbowfish

GOLDFISH

1st Batch	2nd Batch
1 shubunkin	1 black moor
1 red cap oranda	

Introducing New Fish

Your First Batch of Fish

Transporting new fish: When you buy fish, the salesperson will net them and package them into plastic bags for the trip home. Protect the bags from temperature extremes on the way. Do not leave the fish unattended in a hot car in summer or a cold car in winter. Do not place the bags too near the heating and air conditioning ducts, and do not leave the fish bags sitting in direct sunlight. *Caution: Make your fish purchase the* last *purchase of your shopping trip and transport them directly home.*

***Float new arrivals for twenty minutes before releasing them into the new aquarium.

Floating new arrivals: Do not dump your fish directly into the aquarium. Temperature shock may result. Instead, *float the unopened fish bags inside your aquarium for 20 minutes.* This will allow the temperature inside the bag to equalize with the temperature of your tank. *Tip: Turn out the aquarium light to reduce stress while the fish float.*

Releasing the fish: After floating for twenty minutes, you can introduce the fish to your tank. It is usually best not to add the dealer's water to your tank to lessen the chance of introducing disease. Instead, gently net the fish from the bag, let them swim from the net into your aquarium, and discard the dealer's water.

Adding to an Existing Tank

Quarantine: Ideally, you should not add fish to your existing community without first quarantining them for two weeks. This helps prevent the introduction of disease to your currently healthy tank. Sure, a new fish may look quite healthy, but it has been exposed to many pathogens in the dealer's tanks, and may be carrying a latent infection. The stress that the new fish will suffer upon being thrown into a new, unfamiliar community will increase the possibility of it becoming sick.

A quarantine tank can be quite simple and inexpensive. A bare 5 or 10 gallon aquarium with a sponge filter, heater, and a plastic plant or two for cover is all that you need.

When you aren't using your quarantine tank, it can come in quite handy for other uses. Use it as an isolation tank to treat a single sick fish from your aquarium. Use it as a jail for bullies, or to allow time for a beaten fish to heal. A quarantine tank also comes in quite handy for growing out any baby fish that you might discover in the main tank.

Introducing new specimens: Adding fish to an established tank is a little trickier than adding to a new tank, because existing inhabitants have already laid claims to the territory. The new fish may have to fight its way into a territorial claim. If this is a problem, try rearranging all the decorations in the tank. That causes *everyone* to look for a new spot, and puts all on equal footing. Adding a new decoration sometimes helps, too.

New fish are also at extra risk of being eaten. When you open the lid to your aquarium, the next thing your fish expect is for food to hit the water. So, it's not uncommon for a new fish to get bitten as soon as it drops into the tank. To avoid this problem, feed the existing fish first. That way, they won't be interested in food when you introduce the new guy.

Breeding

One fun aspect to the hobby is trying to breed your fish. In some cases, you'll be trying to stop them from breeding! Fish breed in an amazing number of ways. It is beyond the scope of this book to give an in-depth description of the various methods of breeding fish. So, let's touch on some of the highlights, and you can do further research elsewhere.

The easiest breeders are livebearing fishes, which include swordtails, platies, mollies, guppies, and variatus. If you put males and females together, babies will surely result. However, the fry may be eaten by adult tankmates, so provide heavy plantings to give them cover, or move pregnant females to separate hatchery tanks.

Most fish lay eggs. Danios are a prolific fish that scatter non-adhesive eggs that fall to the bottom. They spawn readily in the aquarium, but the eggs and fry are either eaten or sucked up by filters.

Tetras and barbs take egglaying a step further, by scattering adhesive eggs amongst the plants. The plants provide a modicum of protection against marauding egg eaters. The splashing tetra is especially interesting, because it leaps above the water surface to deposit eggs on the underside of overhanging leaves. The male stands guard beneath the eggs, and regularly splashes them to keep them from drying out. The fry—fry are baby fish—fall into the water when they hatch.

Most cichlids lay adhesive eggs on a flat rock or inside a cave. The parents take turns standing guard over the eggs and fry.

Mouthbrooders, such as most cichlids of the African rift lakes, actually carry the eggs in the mouth of one parent. Even after the fry hatch, they dart back into the parent's mouth for protection at the slightest sign of danger! The adult refuses all food while incubating its young.

Bettas and most gouramies build bubblenests by blowing mucous-coated bubbles. Depending on species, the nest may be quite thick. The fish wrap their bodies into a loving embrace and release sperm and eggs, which are then retrieved and blown into the nest of bubbles. The male stands guard until the fry hatch and become free-swimming.

Some fish cheat. At least one species of *Synodontis* catfish darts amongst spawning pairs of African cichlids and gobbles their eggs, while releasing a few of its own. The cichlids become unwitting mouthbrooders to the fry of this catfish!

How to Sex Fish

Livebearers are the easiest to sex. Look for the anal fin—it's the rearmost, lower fin. On females, the fin is a normal fan shape. On males, it is modified to form a tube, called the gonopodium, for transferring sperm to the females. Male livebearers are usually more colorful and smaller than females. Male swordtails even have a fancy sword on the tail. Still, looking for a gonopodium is the only sure way to sex a livebearer.

Sexing egglayers is more problematic. It's different in practically every species. Here are a few general rules:
Barbs and tetras: Males are usually more colorful. Females are usually more heavily bodied. Males of some species have longer fins.
Bettas and gouramies: Males are usually more colorful. Females are usually more heavily bodied.
Cichlids: This is a very diverse group! Males of many species are larger, more colorful, and have longer fins. Some species cannot be sexed at all. There are even African species where the blue males and yellow females appear to be two different species!

Feeding Your Fish

Feeding fish is fun! It's the one time you can truly interact with them. Your fish will soon come running to the glass whenever they see you.

Make *one* person responsible for feeding the fish. Too many cooks turns your aquarium into broth! Either each person expects everyone else to feed—so no one does it—or everyone thinks they are the only one feeding, and the fish get overfed.

Feed twice daily. Set a schedule that works for you. I feed my fish in the morning and then, again, sometime in the evening, after work. Don't forget to consider the eating habits of your fish! If you keep species that only come out at night, offer some food when you turn off the lights.

Feed sparingly. You've probably heard that overfeeding kills the fish. The problem is not that they will overeat. Rather, the problem is that uneaten food decays and pollutes the tank. Feed only what the fish will eat in a maximum of three minutes. If there is still food remaining in the tank at that time, you have overfed.

***Feed only what will be eaten within three minutes. To judge, think of a fish's stomach as being the size of its eye. Most fish require only a couple of flakes per fish, per meal.

It's easier to overfeed than you might think. All it takes is to have more food fall out of the can than you intended. So, never pour the food directly into the tank. Always pour it into your hand first.

In the event that you accidentally overfeed, you must remove the excess. Use your fish net to remove excess food from the surface. Use your gravel vacuum to siphon excess food from the bottom.

Flakes and floating pellets may be sprinkled onto the water surface, after first measuring them into your hand. When you offer tablets or sinking pellets, try to drop them directly in front of the fish you are targeting.

Most freeze-dried foods may also be sprinkled on the water surface. Tubifex worms are a bit more fun to feed, though. The masses of worms come cut into cubes. Reach into the aquarium and press the cube against the inside glass to squeeze out the bubbles. The cube will stick there, where the fish can nibble it.

When feeding frozen foods, most hobbyists simply toss chunks into the water. The fish pick away the bits as they thaw. However, it is probably better to thaw the foods, first.

Rotate foods at each meal to achieve optimal nutrition. Offer several different foods to achieve a varied diet. (Buy small-sized containers to keep them fresh.)

Vacation feeding: If you are going to be away for the weekend, do nothing. The fish will be fine. If you plan to be away longer than that, consider buying "vacation food" which is a plaster block containing embedded food. You drop it into the tank, and it dissolves, releasing food over time.

Daily Duties

Aquariums are really no work at all, but there are some duties to which you must attend each day. Spend a few seconds to do the following:

Turn on the light. You can buy an inexpensive appliance timer which will turn the lights on and off for you, automatically, each day. If you do not have a timer, remember to turn the light off at night to control the growth of algae.

Check the fish. Take a quick peek to make sure everyone looks healthy. Are there any signs of disease? Look for fish that are behaving abnormally. Are any fish missing? Missing fish may be hiding, or may have jumped out. Check the carpet!

Look for deads. Dead fish pollute the aquarium and spread disease. Remove all dead fish immediately. If no other fish show signs of disease, medication is unnecessary. Finding dead fish should be a rare thing.

Check the environment. Make sure the filter is operating, bubblers are bubbling, and the temperature is where it should be.

Feed the fish. Feed two meals per day. Try to offer a different food at each meal to provide the most balanced diet. Keep an eye out for any fish that is off its food.

(Optional) Run water tests. If you are cycling a new aquarium, running daily ammonia and nitrite tests can be very useful.

All the above chores (except running water tests) should take you less than one minute per day to accomplish. A hobby doesn't get any easier than that!

Changing Water

Besides your daily feedings, regular partial water changes are the most important factor to becoming a successful hobbyist. Your fish live in their own toilet. It helps to flush it now and then!

Water changes are essential! Filter systems don't remove all types of waste. Your regular partial water changes remove dissolved wastes that filtration cannot remove. Regular partial water changes replace trace elements that have been depleted by biological activity in the aquarium.

Change 20% of your aquarium water every two weeks.

If you don't, you will lose fish. It may not happen right away, but it will happen. Without regular partial water changes, water quality will degrade over time. Fish are hardy and will tolerate the gradual change up to a limit. When that limit is reached, your fish will die in droves, and there will be no saving them.

In fact, if you go too long without changing water, the water change itself may be lethal! The pH of your aquarium will drop over time—the water will become more acidic. If it gets acidic enough, the helpful bacteria that break down ammonia will quit doing their job. Ammonia will accumulate, but since the pH has dropped so low, the ammonia will not be very toxic. However, when you finally get around to making that long overdue partial water change, it will raise the pH, instantly converting the remaining ammonia into the highly toxic form. You will kiss your fish goodbye.

Small, frequent water changes are better than larger changes done less frequently. Changing 10% or 20% weekly is better yet. Changing 50% monthly is worse.

Using a Gravel Vacuum

The gravel vacuum is the aquarist's best friend. It makes water changes fast and easy. Some would even say that it is fun to use. The device is quite simple, consisting of a siphon hose with a large diameter tube attached at one end. It removes water like a typical siphon hose, but when you push the large end into the gravel, the flow is strong enough to lift out all the detritus, without removing the heavier gravel. It is quite amazing to watch a tornado of crud swirl up the inside of that tube, on its way out of your tank!

To start the gravel vacuum, you need to start it siphoning. Before starting, set a bucket on the floor, next to the aquarium. Submerge the entire hose in your aquarium until there are no bubbles inside it. Then, while keeping the large end underwater, put your thumb over the small end and drop it down into the bucket. Remove your thumb, and the siphon should take right off.

Using the gravel vacuum is easy. While siphoning, simply poke the large end deep into the gravel for a moment. Then, lift. The crud will flow up the tube and the heavier gravel will fall back into the tank. Repeat the procedure—poking and lifting, poking and lifting—cleaning as much gravel as you can while making your 20% water change. If you don't get it all, don't worry. Just take up where you left off at the next partial water change.

Tip: If your gravel is very fine, you may need to pinch the hose, or position your thumb partially over the small end, to slow the flow a bit. You can also use your thumb to temporarily stop the flow, if a fish swims into the vacuum tube.

Cleaning the Filter

Every two weeks, you should change 20% of your water. It's also a good time to check your filter for need of cleaning. Always follow the manufacturer's directions that came with your filter.

Power filters: Power filters are easy to maintain. In most cases, you merely slide out the dirty filter cartridge and replace it with a new clean one.

Filter cartridges are composed of two parts—polyester fiber media and activated carbon. The polyester media collects the bits of solid waste. Activated carbon removes dissolved waste. Filter cartridges may be mounted horizontally or vertically, depending on the brand and model of the filter.

The polyester filter media will become clogged as it collects detritus. As it becomes more clogged, it will restrict flow of water through the filter. When your filter cartridges become clogged, they should be replaced. However, if they are less than a month old, you may be able to rinse them in the sink to restore some functionality.

Tip for hang-on-the-back models: Watch for water to flow into the tank around the intake tube, in addition to flowing out the normal waterfall chute, as a signal that the filter is becoming clogged.

It is not possible to tell when the waste adsorption capability of activated carbon has become depleted. Once those chemical bonds fill up, the activated carbon becomes useless. Worse, a change of pH in your aquarium could cause the activated carbon to release some of those collected wastes back into the aquarium! For this reason, *filter cartridges should always be replaced at least once per month, regardless of how clean they may appear.*

Undergravel filters: With this style of filter, your gravel is the filter media. The filter pulls solid waste into the gravel bed, and traps it there. *Use a gravel vacuum to remove waste from the gravel bed, every two weeks, when you do your regular 20% partial water changes.* If you fail to use a gravel vacuum, the gravel will become clogged and the filter will fail to function.

Some undergravel filters have optional replaceable activated carbon cartridges that fit into the filter exhaust spouts. If your filter uses these, replace them at least once per month. Since these cartridges restrict the flow of water through the exhaust spout, it is really better to remove them and add a small outside power filter to provide chemical filtration.

Most undergravel filters are powered by an air pump that blows air through airstones. As the airstones become clogged—from dust pumped through the airlines, or from algae growing on the outside—it will reduce the bubble output. Check your airstones regularly, and replace them when airflow begins to slow. Clogged airstones put excessive back-pressure on the diaphragm in your air pump and will cause the air pump to wear out prematurely.

If you use powerheads to run your undergravel filter, be sure to check the intake for debris, now and then, and remove any that has collected.

Canister filters: Usually, canister filters sit on the floor. Though they are great filters, they can be a bit of a pain to clean. The easiest style of canister filter hangs on the back of your tank. Maintenance is easier because the filter is easier to reach and there are no hoses to disconnect. This filter uses replaceable media, which may be set up a couple of different ways. One method uses a pleated cartridge that may be rinsed and reused a few times before replacement. The other method uses activated carbon and a polyester filter sleeve. Replace both at cleaning time.

Other Duties

Feeding the fish, changing some water, and cleaning the filter are your primary responsibilities as a hobbyist. These things keep the fish healthy and happy. There are a few chores remaining that will make the human fishkeeper (especially spouses!) happy.

Cleaning the glass: Algae doesn't bother your fish in the least, but we humans find it ugly to look at—especially when it impedes our view of the fish! Use your algae scrubber pad to keep the inside glass clean. Algae growth is different in every type of aquarium, so perform this duty on an as-needed basis. *Warning: Be very careful not get pieces of gravel between the scrubber pad and glass. You will scratch the glass! Acrylic tanks scratch even more easily.* A razor blade may be necessary to remove really tough algae on glass tanks. *Never use a razor blade on acrylic! Remembering to turn your light off at night may help to control future algae problems.*

The outside aquarium glass should be cleaned with a damp paper towel. Feel free to dip a corner into the aquarium to get the towel wet. It is okay to use a window cleaning solution *on the outside glass only,* but it is very dangerous. Window cleaning solutions contain lethal ammonia or pH-altering vinegar. If you use such a product, be extremely careful.

Cleaning decorations: A bit of algae on plastic plants and ceramic decorations does no harm. However, if you would like to clean it away, try removing the decoration to the sink, and scrubbing it with your algae scrubber pad. If that doesn't work, you may add a cup of bleach to a bucket of water and soak the decoration for up to a half hour to kill the algae. Then, scrub again. *Warning: Bleach will kill your fish. Make sure you thoroughly rinse and soak decorations after bleaching them, before returning the decorations to the tank. Bleach may discolor decorations. So, use it at your own risk and as a last resort.*

Pruning plants: If you are keeping live plants, you may need to prune away the excess when they grow. Pinch off the tops of bunch plants, and you can plant the part you pinched off as a new plant.

Cleaning your full-hood: When bubbles burst, they splatter the underside of your light unit. When the splattered water dries, it leaves behind a residue from dissolved minerals. These mineral deposits may build up and become unsightly. Remove the hood and scrub with a toothbrush to remove the deposits. In extreme cases, try scrubbing with some vinegar to help loosen them. Be very careful not to get vinegar in the aquarium!

Splatters under the light may stay wet long enough to foster algae growth. Your algae scrubber pad should make short work of this algae. If not, use a single-edge razor blade to scrape the algae and mineral residue away from the glass on the underside of the light unit.

Changing bulbs: When incandescent bulbs burn out, you know it, but fluorescent bulbs wind down before they burn out. Though a fluorescent bulb will light for up to three years, it is best to change them every year or so, because they lose intensity as they age.

Air pump maintenance: Some air pumps have a felt filter on the underside. Clean or replace it as needed. Run a paper clip through the openings of gang-valves, occasionally, to clear any blockages.

Heater maintenance: Aside from wiping off the housing, there is little maintenance on a heater. Check regularly to be sure no water has entered the heater tube.

Aquarium stand: Dust as needed. Consider using a furniture polish.

Stress & Disease

Stress is the main cause of problems in your tank. Even the word itself—"dis-ease"—means stress. Yes, germs cause disease, but germs are everywhere, and stress is what makes a fish susceptible to them.

The same things that stress us stress a fish: bullying, incompatibility, foul water, lack of oxygen, lack of rest, loud noises, improper diet, crowding, lack of privacy, and so forth. Your actions in providing the proper environment for your fish are what prevent disease.

Signs of Ill Health

First, look for stress:
- Has a fish lost its color?
- Is a normally active fish suddenly hiding?
- Is there weight loss?
- Is the fish's breathing excessively rapid?
- Is it gasping at the water surface?
- Are there clamped fins? (fins folded against the body)
- Is the fish shimmying in place?

Then, look for signs of infection:
- Are there white dots on the fish (as if someone sprinkled it from a salt shaker)?
- Are there white slimy patches on the skin or fins?
- Are there bloody patches or bloody streaks present?
- Do the fins look ragged or decayed?
- Does the mouth look cottony?
- Do the eyes look cloudy?
- Are there any light fuzzy patches on body or fins?

Signs of stress are signs of warning. Corrective action must be taken—usually improvements to water quality—or disease will result. Disease must be medicated.

Medication Tips

Before treating with any medication:
- Run ammonia, nitrite, and pH tests to be sure the water quality is within acceptable bounds.
- If you have not kept up with your regular partial water changes, change some water before treatment.
- Remove activated carbon from the filter system during treatment. It will remove many medications. Do not turn off the filter!
- Follow the manufacturer's instructions for dosage.
- Consider keeping 1-2 teaspoons of aquarium salt per gallon of water during treatment to boost healing.

There are many brand names of medicine on the market. Most use standard ingredients and slap on a proprietary name. This can be confusing because two seemingly different products may actually be the exact same thing! You will do best if you ignore brand names and look for the active ingredients. Both active ingredients and common brand names are listed in the treatments below.

Diseases & Treatments

Protozoal infections:

•**Ich**, named after the parasite that causes it, *Ichthyophthirius multifilius,* and pronounced "ick," is easy to spot. It forms tiny white dots on the body and fins, making the fish appear to have been sprinkled from a salt shaker. Ich is easy to treat. If you catch the infection early, you shouldn't lose any fish to it. Without treatment, lethal skin and gill damage will result. **Note:** Standard medication will not kill the parasites on the fish. It only kills them when they drop off to multiply. So, always treat at least one day past the disappearance of dots to eliminate the parasite. Typical treatment is three to four days, but may vary.

•**Velvet disease** is a little harder to spot. The parasites are smaller than ich and cause a gentle dusting on the fish, which may give a velvety sheen, especially when viewed at an angle to the light. Treatment may take two weeks or more.

Treating protozoal infections: Use malachite green (*Nox-Ich®*), or a combination of formalin and malachite green (*QuickCure®*), to treat ich, velvet, and other protozoal infections. The formalin and malachite green combo is a bit stronger, but harder on live aquatic plants. Treatment with copper sulfate (*Aquarisol®*) may also be useful.

***Life cycle of the ich parasite.

Bacterial infections:
•**Fin rot** appears as ragged edges to the fins, with a white or gray edge. Decay may be rapid. Please note that a white or gray trim to the edge of the fin is normal for some species! Know your fish! Treat with antibiotics. If fins are ragged from a nip, but don't have the grayed edge, they should heal unaided.
•**Cloudy eyes** are usually the result of poor water quality, particularly low pH or high ammonia levels.
•**Mouth rot** or "mouth fungus" is caused by bacteria, not fungi. The symptoms present as a white, or cottony, fringe to the lips. Treat with an antibiotic.

•**Open sores** or **slimy patches** on the body usually denote bacterial infections, but may also represent advanced infections from protozoans and flukes. In most cases, an antibiotic treatment is all that is in order, but you may want to combine with a treatment for protozoans.

> **Treating bacterial infections:** Use an antibiotic. Some antibiotics are better than others. Look for antibiotics containing these active ingredients: "furan" drugs (furazolidone, nitrofurazone, etc.) (*Furan-2®, Furanace®, Fungus Eliminator®*), sulfa drugs (such as sulfamethazine and sulfathiozole) (*Tri-Sulfa®*), kanamycin, or minocycline (*Maracyn 2®*). Less effective choices include penicillin, erythromycin (*Maracyn®*), and tetracycline.

True fungal infections:
•**Fuzzy growths** on the body or fins represent true fungus. It's the thick, moldy-looking growth, like you find growing on dead fish. Many bacterial diseases are mistakenly called "fungus" and require antibiotic treatment. Don't be confused. True fungus won't infect a healthy fish, ever, because it attacks only dead tissue. It is a secondary infection. True fungus gets a foothold when other disease or injury progresses to advanced stages, leaving dead tissue behind.

> **Treating true fungus:** Paint the wound with methylene blue or mercurochrome daily, until cured, or treat with a *MarOxy®*. Combine with an antibiotic for added benefit.

Viral infections:
•**Lymphocystis** is the only readily recognizable viral infection. The disease starts as white, ich-like dots, usually on the edge of fins. As it progresses, the dots grow into cauliflower-like lumps. Viral infections, including lymphocystis, are not treatable. The good news is that the fish may eventually heal on its own. *Caution: This disease is commonly seen on painted glassfish.*

Worms and flukes:
•Parasitic worms may infect fish. Unfortunately, it's nearly impossible to diagnose these infections without aid of a microscope and autopsies. Treat with organophosphate medication, such as *Clout®*.

Algae Control

The theme in *Jurassic Park* was that "life finds a way." If your aquarium has light and nutrients, something green will find a way to use them. Sometimes the combination of light and nutrients allows green growth to get out of hand, resulting in ugly algae.

The intensity and spectrum of light on every tank is different. The nutrients in local tapwater vary, and that doesn't count the nutrients added when you feed the fish! Even the pH and hardness of the water is a factor. So, it is sometimes hard to predict where algae will occur.

There are different kinds of algae. Single-celled, free-floating algae turn the water a soupy green. Algae can grow as slime on the glass, or as hair on the rocks. It can be green, brown, or even red. You may even stumble across blue-green algae, which is not an algae at all, but a cyanobacterial film!

Because there are so many types of algae and conditions that can cause it, algae control can be a tricky thing. Luckily, most cases are minor and involve an occasional wiping of the glass to keep the view clear. An occasional scrubbing of rocks with a toothbrush may also be necessary. Chemical algicides should only be used as a last resort—they contain poisons that may harm plants or fish.

Algae prevention:
- Feed carefully. Overfeeding provides nutrients for algae.
- Turn off lights at night. Your fish need rest and they have no eyelids!
- Keep algae-eating fish such as plecostomus and otocinclus. The Chinese algae-eater is a poor choice, as it tends to attack the other fish when larger.
- Grow live aquatic plants. Plants are more efficient at utilizing nutrients and tend to starve out algae. Note: It will take more than one or two plants, though!

Aggression

Bad fish…bad fish…whatcha gonna do? Sometimes, fish fight. Most spats are minor and need no attention. No damage is done. Then, there are those other times…

In the section on compatibility, we talked about why fish fight, and how to choose fish that get along. In the section on introducing new fish, we talked about how to give new arrivals a fighting chance at fitting into a new community.

Still, even taking the best precautions, fights may ensue. After all, things change. Fish grow up. They want more territory. They decide to take a mate. These are reasons that can make a formerly peaceful fish become a fish that suddenly attacks.

Again, most attacks are minor—more threat than attack—and can be ignored. But when things get out of hand, you must step in. If one fish is doing all the fin-kicking, remove that fish from the community. Perhaps you have another tank where it will better fit in. Or, place the offender in an isolation tank. You can also hang a net breeder in the main aquarium and isolate the fish there.

Whenever possible, remove the offending party. Removing the injured party only reinforces the behavior, and the bad fish will likely stalk a new victim. Also be aware that removing the head bad guy may just allow another fish to move up the pecking order. Dethroned dictators may be replaced by someone just as bad.

If the victim is badly beaten, it must be separated from the other fish. Fish spot weakness and harass an injured fish. They will pick at its wounds, its eyes, and its fins. The poor fish won't get a chance to heal. As long as infection is not evident, the fish may be placed in a net breeder for healing. Otherwise, remove it to a separate treatment tank for medication.

Resources

This book contains all the basics for setting up and running a successful aquarium, but there is lots more to learn! So, don't stop here. The following resources will help you delve deeper into your new hobby. Happy fishkeeping!

Aquarium Books

KISS Guide to Freshwater Aquariums (Keep It Simple Series), Mike Wickham, Dorling Kindersley Publishing, 2000
KISS Guide to Saltwater Aquariums (Keep It Simple Series), Mike Wickham, Dorling Kindersley Publishing, 2000
The New Aquarium Handbook, Ines Scheurmann, Barron's Educational Series, 1986
Aquarium Atlas (Volumes 1-5), Hans A. Baensch and Dr. Rudiger Riehl, Microcosm, 1997
Dr. Axelrod's Atlas of Freshwater Aquarium Fishes (9th Edition), Dr. Herbert Axelrod, et al, T.F.H. Publications, 1997

Hobby Magazines

Aquarium Fish Magazine, Fancy Publications, P. O. Box 53351, Boulder, CO, 80322; monthly; www.aquariumfish.com
Tropical Fish Hobbyist, T.F.H. Publications, One TFH Plaza, Neptune City, NJ, 07753; monthly; www.tfh.com
Freshwater and Marine Aquarium, R/C Modeler Corp., P. O. Box 487, Sierra Madre, CA, 91025; monthly; www.mag-web.com/fama/
Practical Fishkeeping, Motorsport, 550 Honey Locust Rd., Jonesburg, MO, 63351; bimonthly

Aquarium Societies

Aquarium clubs exist throughout North America and the United Kingdom. Joining a local club lets you meet fellow hobbyists, attend lectures given by recognized experts, learn tips and tricks, and make friends with people who share your interests. Contact the following organizations for the location of a club near you:

Federation of American Aquarium Societies
4816 E. 64th St.
Indianapolis, IN 46220-4728
Tel: (317) 255-2523

Canadian Association of Aquarium Clubs
298 Creighton Court
Waterloo, Ontario
Canada N2K 1W6

Web Sites

The Internet and the World Wide Web put a wealth of information at your fingertips. Unfortunately, the information may be quite scattered and links come and go. Here are some popular links that have been around for a while. Search engines, such as *google*, *northernlight*, and *yahoo* may steer you toward other interesting sites.

http://go.compuserve.com/fishnet (CompuServe members use: GO FISHNET) This is the author's favorite site!
http://www.aol.com
   (AOL members use KEYWORD: PET CARE)
http://www.petsforum.com/csi
http://www.aqualink.com
http://www.actwin.com/fish/index.cgi
http://www.fishlinkcentral.com/
http://www.thekrib.com
http://www.tetra-fish.com
http://www.aquariainc.com
http://www.animal-graphics.com
http://www.walmart.com
http://www.dalmatianpress.com

Public Aquariums

Public aquariums (fish zoos) offer a great learning experience. Besides seeing aquatic life that you can't keep in a home aquarium, such as dolphins and penguins, you'll also get to see some typical aquarium fish at full-blown adult size! See the three-foot long version of that pacu you just bought! Here are some of the country's more well-known public aquariums:

New York Aquarium
Boardwalk and West 8th St.
Brooklyn, NY 11224

National Aquarium in Baltimore
Pier 3, 501 E. Pratt St.
Baltimore, MD 21202

John G. Shedd Aquarium
1200 S. Lake Shore Dr.
Chicago, IL 60605

Monterey Bay Aquarium
886 Cannery Row
Monterey, CA 93940

The Florida Aquarium
Harbour Island
Tampa, FL 33602

Aquarium of the Americas
Woldenberg Riverfront Park
New Orleans, LA 70130

Waikiki Aquarium
2777 Kalakaua Ave
Honolulu, HI 96815